TIMELINES
OF ANCIENT CIVILIZATIONS

AZTECS

David and Patricia Armentrout

Newbridge

Aztecs
ISBN 1-4007-4133-5

Written by David and Patricia Armentrout

Published by Sundance/Newbridge Educational Publishing, LLC,
A Haights Cross Communications Company
11 East 26th Street, New York, NY 10010
www.newbridgeonline.com

Title Page: *The Aztec calendar stone was discovered in 1760, buried in the main square in Mexico City.*

PHOTO CREDITS:© Corel Corporation p 8, 12; © Getty Images p 6;
© Library of Congress pp 10, 21, 25; © IRC-www.historypictures.com Cover, pp
22, 27; © Philip Baird/www.anthroarcheart.org Title, pp 14, 18; © Hulton/Archive
by Getty Images p 16; © Map by Artville

10 9 8 7 6 5 4 3 2 1

Contents

AD 1111

THE AZTECS SEARCH FOR A NEW HOME

Not much is known about the Aztec people before the 12th century AD. Ancient Aztec stories and myths tell of a land called Aztlán. The stories explain that Aztlán was the original home of the Aztec people. **Archaeologists** and historians believe Aztlán was located somewhere in northern Mexico. In the year AD 1111, the Aztecs left Aztlán in search of a better home. They wandered for many years.

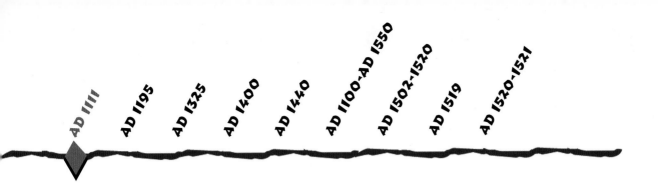

AD 1111   AD 1195   AD 1325   AD 1400   AD 1440   AD 1100-AD 1550   AD 1502-1520   AD 1519   AD 1520-1521

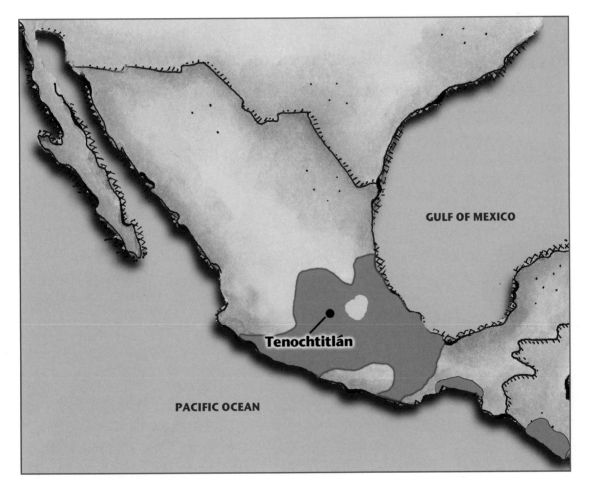

GULF OF MEXICO

Tenochtitlán

PACIFIC OCEAN

The brown shading shows the extent of the Aztec Empire.

AD 1195

THE AZTECS SETTLE IN THE VALLEY OF MEXICO

In AD 1195, the Aztecs stumbled into the Valley of Mexico and decided to settle there.

According to legend, the Aztec Empire began with a **vision**. An eagle appeared. It perched on top of a cactus that grew from a rock in a lake. The eagle was eating a snake it held in its talons. The Aztecs were to build their great city on that very spot.

The Aztecs built an **empire**. At its peak, the Aztec Empire may have had nearly five million citizens.

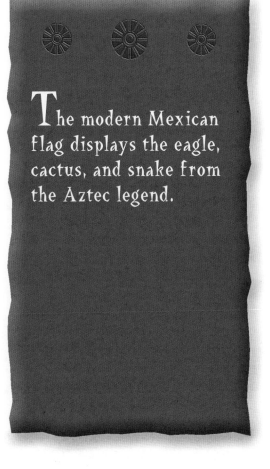

The modern Mexican flag displays the eagle, cactus, and snake from the Aztec legend.

The Mexican flag proudly displays Aztec symbols.

AD 1325

TENOCHTITLAN

Around AD 1325, the Aztecs began building a city on an island in the middle of a swampy lake. The city would be called Tenochtitlán. In time, it would become one of the largest cities in the world.

Aztec engineers built three **causeways** made of earth and stone that connected the island to the mainland. Bridges built into the causeways could be removed to keep invaders from reaching the city. People traveled by canoe along the many canals that wound through the city.

The modern capital of Mexico, Mexico City, is built on top of the ancient site of Tenochtitlán. Just as Tenochtitlán was, Mexico City is one of the largest cities in the world.

An Aztec temple was unearthed by construction workers in Mexico City.

AZTEC FAMILY LIFE

By the early 15th century, the Aztec Empire was growing strong. As Aztec power and wealth grew, their society developed quickly.

Family life was important in Aztec society. Each family member had a job. Children learned from an early age that hard work was expected from everyone.

A page from an ancient book shows Aztec people farming and socializing.

Aztec parents were strict, and a child who misbehaved was punished severely. One form of punishment was to be pricked with the spines of a cactus. Ouch!

Boys attended school. They learned to be warriors. They were also taught a craft or skill. Unless a girl came from a **noble** family, she did not attend school. Girls were taught at home by their mothers.

Wealthy Aztecs drank a chocolate drink called chocolatl made from crushed cocoa beans. Cocoa beans were so valuable that they were also used as money.

11

AD 1440

ISLAND GARDENS

Much of the land around Tenochtitlán was swampy and unfit for farming. Aztec engineers and farmers built small island gardens called chinampas. Chinampas were built by piling up mud from the lake bottom. These meant the Aztecs could grow food.

Crops grew well in the fertile soil. Farmers grew corn, beans, chili peppers, and sweet potatoes.

In AD 1440, Montezuma I ruled the Aztec empire. Montezuma I ordered new and larger chinampas to be built. The new chinampas were designed to control water, grow crops, and provide canals for transportation. Some of these chinampas can still be seen today.

The Aztecs sometimes added meat or vegetables to flour tortillas. Can you guess what they were called? Tacos.

The remains of Aztec chinampas can still be visited near Mexico City.

AD 1440

AZTEC SPORTS

The Aztecs enjoyed sports. One favorite sport was called tlachtli. A team had four or five players. Two teams played on a stone court surrounded by high walls. The object of the game was to get a small rubber ball through a stone ring set high on the wall.

Players were only allowed to touch the ball with their thighs, hips, or elbows. The game often became quite rough.

Teams had good reason for playing hard. Losers were sometimes sacrificed, or killed, as a **tribute** to the gods.

The Aztecs made rubber out of sap from rubber trees.

An ancient ball court used by the Aztecs

READING AND WRITING

The Aztecs did not have a way to write down words. Instead, they drew pictures called **glyphs**. The Aztecs used this system of picture writing for most of their known history.

Certain glyphs had special meanings. A club and shield meant war. A footprint stood for travel.

The Aztecs used picture symbols called glyphs to mark buildings and sculptures.

Trained glyph writers were known as scribes. They could record an entire story by drawing glyphs. Once a story was completed, the series of glyphs were folded together like a book. An Aztec book was called a **codex**.

Aztec scribes drew pictures on paper called amatl. Amatl was made from the bark of trees or from animal skins.

AD 1100-AD 1550

THE AZTEC CALENDAR

The Aztecs used two different calendars to mark the passage of time. The sacred calendar had 260 days a year. Each day had a special symbol, or glyph. Each glyph had a different meaning. The Aztecs used the calendar to plan for the future.

The sun calendar had 365 days a year. It was used to keep track of the seasons. The sun calendar had five days that were considered to be unlucky by Aztec priests.

Once every 52 years, the first day of both calendars was the same. This was considered to be the beginning of a new age, or cycle.

The Aztec Calendar Stone, or Sun Stone, found near Mexico City, weighs more than 20 tons.

19

AZTEC RELIGION

Aztecs were religious people. They believed gods controlled everything in their lives. The Aztecs had many harsh customs and beliefs. They believed their gods demanded human sacrifice.

The Aztecs' most important god was the god of war. He was also the sun god. The god of war demanded human blood in return for his protection. Enemy warriors captured in battle were often killed or sacrificed by Aztec priests. The blood of the warriors was offered to the god of war.

The Aztecs thought sacrifices made to the gods would protect them from harm. It was not uncommon for thousands of prisoners to be sacrificed in a single ceremony.

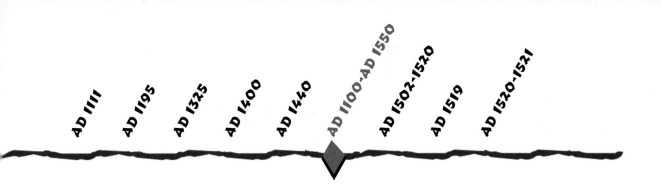

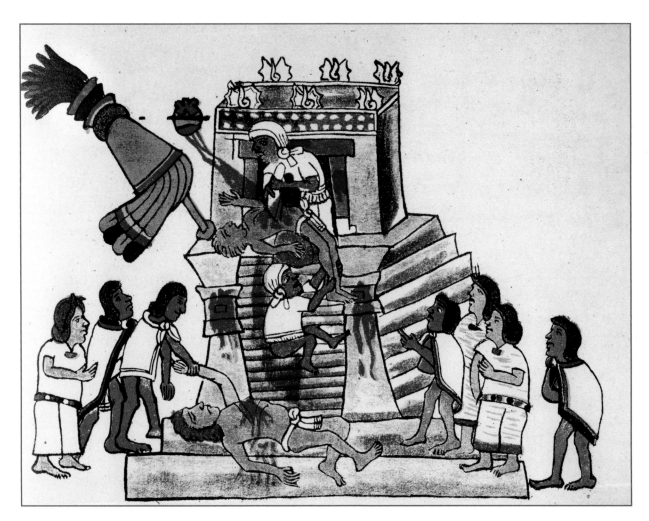

The Aztecs sacrificed humans to win favor with the gods.

AD 1502-1520

MONTEZUMA II

Montezuma II became the emperor of the Aztecs in 1502. At that time the Aztec empire was the largest and most powerful in **Mesoamerica**.

The Aztec emperor Montezuma II ruled over a large empire.

Montezuma II had been a warrior and then high priest before being crowned emperor. He directed many successful battles against neighboring tribes. When the Aztecs conquered a tribe, they demanded tribute (a sort of tax) to be paid. If the tribe refused to pay tribute, they would be attacked. In this way, the Aztecs grew stronger and wealthier.

AD 1519

THE SPANISH ARRIVE

In 1519, strangers arrived in the Aztec lands. The Aztec king Montezuma II may have thought the white men with beards were gods. The white men were Spanish **conquistadors** led by Hernán Cortés.

At first, the conquistadors were treated well. Still, Cortés believed he and his men were at risk and decided to take Montezuma hostage. The conquistadors saw that the Aztecs had gold and other treasures. They wanted it for themselves and for the king of Spain. Cortés and his men took much of the gold. A group of Aztec warriors tried to stop the Spanish. There was a battle and the Spanish soldiers killed many Aztecs.

Montezuma greets Spanish conquistador Hernán Cortés.

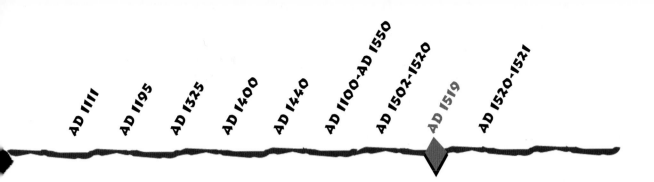

THE FALL OF TENOCHTITLAN

Montezuma II died in 1520. He was killed, either by the Spanish or by Aztecs who were unhappy with his leadership. Soon war broke out. The conquistadors were helped in battle by Indian tribes that hated the Aztecs. The conquistadors and their **allies** attacked Tenochtitlán. Thousands died during the many battles.

In 1521, after a long battle, Cortés and his men captured the capital city of Tenochtitlán. The rule of the Aztecs was over.

Tenochtitlán was renamed Mexico City. The King of Spain called the area we know as Mexico, New Spain. Cortés was named the governor of the new Spanish colony. Today, Aztec **descendants** still live in Mexico.

Hernán Cortés became the governor of New Spain.

27

Timeline

Aztec legends state the Aztec people lived in an area known as Aztlán, located somewhere in northwest Mexico, before AD 1100.

AD 1111
The Aztecs leave Aztlán in search of a new home

AD 1325
The Aztecs begin building the city of Tenochtitlán

AD 1502
Montezuma II becomes ruler

AD 1195
The Aztecs reach the Valley of Mexico

AD 1440
Montezuma I begins his rule

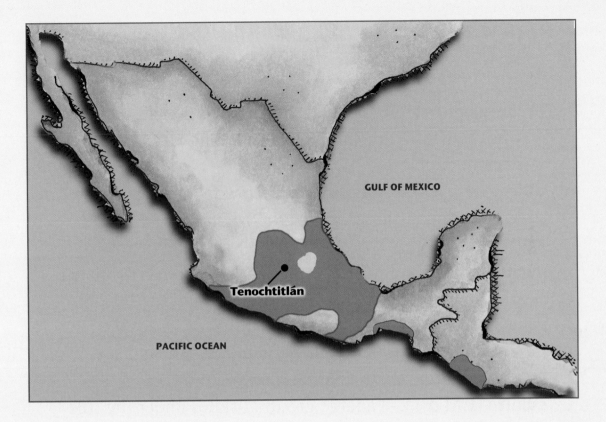

GULF OF MEXICO

Tenochtitlán

PACIFIC OCEAN

AD 1520
*Montezuma II
is killed*

AD 1522
*Cortés is named
governor of New Spain*

AD 1519
*Cortés
arrives in
land of
Mexico*

AD 1521
*Cortés attacks and
destroys Tenochtitlán*

GLOSSARY

archaeologists (AR kee AHL uh jests) — people
who study past human life by examining artifacts left by
ancient people

allies (AL eyes) — groups of people who join together
for a common cause

causeways (KAWZ wayz) — raised roads built across water

conquistadors (kuhn KEES tuh dorz) — Spanish soldiers
who conquered the New World

codex (KOH dex) — an Aztec book

descendants (di SEND uhnts) — your descendants are
your children, their children, and so on

empire (EM pyr) — a large group of states under the rule
of one person

glyphs (GLIFS) — picture symbols

Mesoamerica (MES oh uh MAIR eh kuh) — a word used
by archaeologists that describes the region and cultures
in Mexico and parts of Central America before the
Spanish conquest

noble (NO bul) — from a high-ranking family

tribute (TRIB yoot) — a gift to a king or god

vision (VIZH uhn) — something that is imagined or
dreamed about

PRONUNCIATION GUIDE

amatl (ah MAH tl)
Aztlán (ast LAHN)
chinampas (chin AHM pas)
chocolatl (cho ko LAH tl)
Montezuma (mahn tuh ZOO muh)
Tenochtitlán (tay noch teet LAHN)
Tlachtli (TLOCH tlee)

FURTHER READING

Barghusen, Joan D. *The Aztecs: End of a Civilization.*
    Lucent Books 2000

Rees, Rosemary. *The Aztecs.* Heinemann Library 1999

WEBSITES TO VISIT

http://home.freeuk.com/elloughton13/mexico.htm
www.kidskonnect.com/Mexico/MexicoHome.html

INDEX

ABOUT THE AUTHORS

David and Patricia Armentrout have written many nonfiction
books for young readers. They have had several books
published for primary school reading. The Armentrouts live
in Cincinnati, Ohio, with their two children.